Life in a

TREE

Clare Oliver

RAINTREE
STECK-VAUGHN
PUBLISHERS

A Harcourt Company

Austin   New York
www.raintreesteckvaughn.com

Published by Raintree Steck-Vaughn Publishers, an imprint of Steck-Vaughn Company.

Project Editors: Sean Dolan and Tamsin Osler
Production Director: Richard Johnson
Illustrated by Stuart Lafford
Designed by Ian Winton

Planned and produced by Discovery Books

Library of Congress Cataloging-in-Publication Data

Oliver, Clare.
Life in a tree/Clare Oliver.
p.cm. -- (Microhabitats)
Includes bibliographical references (p.).
ISBN 0-7398-4334-6
1. Forest animals--Juvenile literature. 2. Forest ecology--Juvenile literature. 3. Trees--Ecology--Juvenile literature.
[1. Trees--Ecology. 2.Forest ecology. 3. Ecology.] I. Title.

QL112 .045 2001
577.3--dc21

2001019550

Printed and bound in the United States
1 2 3 4 5 6 7 8 9 LB 07 06 05 04 03 02

Acknowledgments
The publishers would like to thank the following for permission to reproduce their pictures:
Front cover: Kim Taylor/Bruce Coleman Collection; p.7: P. Kaya/Oxford Scientific Films; p.9: Gordon
Maclean/Oxford Scientific Films; p.10: N.A. Callow/Natural History Photographic Agency; p.11t: Chris
Fairclough/Discovery Picture Library; p.11b: Tim Shepherd/Oxford Scientific Films; p.12t: Stephen Dalton/Natural
History Photographic Agency; p.12b: Jane Burton/Bruce Coleman Collection; p.13: PhotoLink/PhotoDisc; p.14: Hans
Reinhard/Bruce Coleman Collection; p.15: Richard Day/Oxford Scientific Films; p.16: David Wright/Oxford Scientific
Films; p.17: Andrew Purcell/Bruce Coleman Collection; p.18: Kim Taylor/Bruce Coleman Collection; p.19: Kim
Taylor/Bruce Coleman Collection; p.20: Jane Burton/Bruce Coleman Collection; p.21: Hans Reinhard/Bruce Coleman
Collection; p.22: G.I. Bernard/Oxford Scientific Films; p.23: Chris Fairclough Picture Library;
p.24: PhotoLink/PhotoDisc; p.25t: PhotoLink/Photodisc; p.25b: Chris Fairclough Picture Library;
p.26t: Dr. Eckart Pott/Bruce Coleman Collection; p.26b: William S. Paton/Bruce Coleman Collection;
p.27: PhotoLink/PhotoDisc; p.28: Terry Heathcote/Oxford Scientific Films; p.29: Malcolm Penny.

Contents

Life in a Tree 4

Animal Life 12

Web of Life 20

Other Trees 24

The Importance of Trees 28

Glossary 30

Further Reading and Websites 31

Index 32

Life in a Tree

The Oak Tree

All trees are amazing microhabitats—an almost self-contained small environment. This book looks at the rich diversity of plants and animals that live in or near the oak tree, a typical broadleaved tree that grows naturally throughout North America, Europe, and Asia, as well as northern parts of South America and North Africa.

Wasp

There are over 450 different **species** of oak. Oaks can be deciduous or evergreen. Most oaks are huge trees that can live for hundreds of years. They easily grow as tall as an eight-story building. The trunk is usually too wide to stretch your arms around—its circumference can be more than 10 yards (9 m)! Oaks need sunlight to grow and do not do well in the shade.

Bark beetle

Gray squirrel

Barn owl

Guess What?

A tree's rings reveal what has happened in the tree's environment—including plagues, fires, and droughts.

A full-grown tree can manufacture 5 pounds of pure oxygen per day. An acre of trees can remove 13 tons of dust per year.

A full-grown tree can provide the cooling equivalent of 10 room-size air conditioning units.

Vaporer moth caterpillar

Rabbit

Many different kinds of birds perch on the branches of the oak tree. Squirrels and other mammals scurry along the branches or nest in the leaf litter. The thick, gnarled trunk supports fungi, ivy, and thousands of insects and spiders.

From Little Acorns...

The oak tree starts life as a little acorn, which is the fruit or nut of the adult oak tree. In autumn the acorns drop to the ground, where some of them are eaten by animals and birds. Or they may be collected and buried by squirrels and jays, as an underground food supply for the bleak winter months. But sometimes these animals forget to come back. This gives the acorns a fine start on new life. They have been taken a little distance from the shadow of the parent tree and buried to the right depth in the soil. They now have a chance to grow on their own.

A tree trunk grows fatter every year by adding a new ring of wood under the bark. By counting these rings, it is possible to calculate a tree's age.

Growth ring produced every year

Heartwood

Bark

Life Begins

When spring arrives in **temperate** climates, the Earth is warmed by the Sun and watered by rain. The warmth and moisture help the acorn to **germinate**. It produces a shoot that will grow into the trunk, split off to make branches, and sprout leaves.

It is hard to believe that this seedling may grow into an oak tree 90 feet (27 m) tall.

The acorn also produces a root. This will grow into an underground network of roots that supports the tree and sucks up water and nutrients from the Earth.

Spring into Summer

Most oaks are deciduous. This means that they grow fresh leaves each spring and shed them in the autumn. In spring, the oak tree bursts into life again. Its bare branches sprout hundreds of buds that open into shiny green leaves.

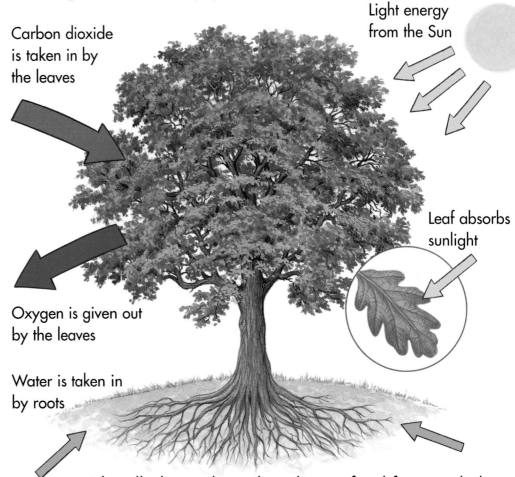

Carbon dioxide is taken in by the leaves

Light energy from the Sun

Leaf absorbs sunlight

Oxygen is given out by the leaves

Water is taken in by roots

Like all plants, the oak makes its food from sunlight. The chlorophyll in the leaves uses energy from sunlight, water from the soil, and carbon dioxide from the air to make the sugars and starch needed to feed the tree.

Blowing in the Wind

At about the same time, the tree produces flowers. Each oak tree bears two types of flowers, or catkins—male and female. The oak relies on the wind to blow the tiny grains of pollen from the male flowers onto the female flowers. In this way, the female flowers are **fertilized**. An acorn starts to develop from each fertilized flower. The overlapping scales at the base of the flower become the tough cup that holds the acorn.

The male flowers are usually scraggly, greenish-yellow catkins that dangle in bunches below the leaves. The tiny female flowers grow singly or in spiky clusters at the tips of the twigs and branches.

See for Yourself

Each kind of oak tree has a different-shaped leaf. Some have stalks; some do not. Some have jagged lobes; some have smooth lobes. How many different kinds can you find?

Autumn and Winter

In autumn, the deciduous oak tree gets ready for the winter. It starts to shed its leaves. The precious green pigment, or coloring, called chlorophyll, which helps the tree make food, is broken down chemically. The useful parts are sucked back into the twigs and branches to be used by the next year's leaves.

Without their green pigment, the leaves turn orange, red, yellow, or even purple. Finally, they dry out and turn brown.

An oak tree may lose as many as 250,000 leaves in autumn.

The dead leaves are blown down to the ground. There they rot to make rich leaf litter, which returns the **nutrients** to the soil. By now the ripe acorns have fallen to the ground. Those that are not eaten by hungry animals will spend the winter in a **dormant** state.

In winter the ground under an oak tree is covered with dead leaves, acorns, and twigs.

By the time midwinter comes, the oak's branches are bare, but its thick bark protects the tree from the cold.

Animal Life

Mammals

Mammals are warm-blooded animals that feed their babies on mother's milk and are often covered in soft fur or hair. Lots of different mammals live in or near the shelter of the oak tree.

Bats roost in hollows in the trunks of old oak trees. They come out at night to hunt for insects.

Food and Shelter

Mice and squirrels (below) eat the oak tree's young shoots in spring and then its juicy acorns in autumn. Deer find acorns to be a tasty treat, too. Mice and

voles may make their nests at the foot of the tree, among the gnarly old roots. For warmth, they line their nests with shed fur and fallen leaves.

Walls and Ceilings

The tree's thick roots provide natural walls and ceilings for mice and voles that dig in the gaps between them to make their homes. Bigger mammals—such as rabbits, badgers, raccoons, and foxes—make their warrens, sets, burrows, and dens here, too. Some, like the badger, sleep there in the winter months.

Guess What?

Squirrels live in tree hollows or build nests, called dreys, out of oak leaves and twigs.

The American badger—a burrowing mammal related to the weasel—has powerful front paws that can dig faster than a man can with a spade.

A red fox trots through the snow in a forest clearing in search of food.

Birds

Many different types of bird, including the woodpecker and magpie, make their nests in the oak tree. The birds get a home, but the tree benefits, too. Bird droppings are an extra source of nutrients, helping to feed the tree.

Like bats, barn owls often roost in oak trees during the day.

Bed and Breakfast in the Oak

Some birds only visit the oak to rest or for a meal. Acorns provide food for crows, rooks, jays, and wood pigeons. Wood pigeons can eat as many as 120 acorns in a day! Crows, rooks, and jays also eat insects that live in the tree, and they may prey on other smaller birds.

Warblers and house wrens may stop by to gulp down a juicy caterpillar or two. These songbirds are known for their sweet voices. Many other songbirds, such as the robin and wood thrush, may perch high in the oak's branches and sing to attract a mate.

House wrens like to make their nests in the holes or recesses of a tree.

See for Yourself

If you spot little holes in a tree trunk, each containing an acorn, that's a sign that the acorn woodpecker is nearby! It may drill hundreds of storage holes, tapping them out with its beak.

If you find a neat little pellet of bones and feathers or fur under an oak tree, you can be sure that an owl has been in the tree. Owls swallow their prey whole, then cough up a pellet.

This feather belongs to a pheasant. You can tell because it is long and colorful, with banded markings along its length.

15

Crawling Creatures

As many as 500 species of insects and bugs depend on the oak tree for food. Underground, the larvae, or grubs, of click beetles munch through the roots. Above ground, in the litter of leaves at the base of the tree, wood lice can usually be found.

Bark and Branches

Bark lice clamber over the tree's bark, while borer beetles gnaw patterns into the wood beneath it. The oak's leaves are eaten by hungry stink bugs. In autumn, weevils drill into the acorns with their long "snouts" to get at the sweet kernel inside.

Weevils, like the one feeding on an acorn above, belong to the insect order Coleoptera, which also includes the beetles.

Insect Eggs

Some weevils lay their eggs inside acorns, while other insects lay their eggs just under the bark. Where this happens, the oak produces a gall—a kind of swollen scab, sometimes with a hard layer that protects the insects inside.

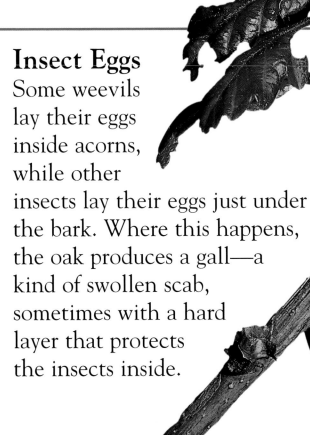

Oak apple galls are caused by the tiny gall wasp. A large oak apple might contain 30 wasp grubs.

See for Yourself

Look out for these orange spots on the underside of oak leaves. These are called spangle galls, and inside each one is the grub of a wasp.

Look for holes in an oak apple gall from which fully grown gall wasps have emerged.

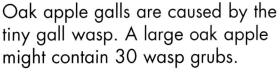

Butterflies and Moths

Butterflies and moths often lay their eggs on the leaves of the oak tree. That way, when the caterpillars hatch, they'll have lots of juicy leaves to eat! Big caterpillars munch right through the leaf, but some caterpillars are so small that they only make tiny tunnels between the top and bottom surfaces of the leaf.

Moth caterpillars, such as those of the vaporer moth, can strip an oak tree of its leaves.

A tortoiseshell butterfly.

These mottled umber moths are well camouflaged among dead oak leaves.

Guess What?

Can you guess what carpenter moth caterpillars eat? The name gives you a clue: wood.

Sometimes oak trees lose so many leaves to hungry caterpillars that they have to sprout a second set of leaves.

Micromoths are so tiny, having a wingspan of just over 0.5 of an inch (2 cm), that it is easy for them to hide in cracks in oak bark.

Woodland Moths

Woodland moths are colored to blend in with their surroundings. Moths that rest on leaves are usually some shade of green. Those that rest on tree trunks are often mottled brown.

Web of Life

The Hunters and the Hunted

Juicy caterpillars that feed on the oak tree attract hunters that feed on them! The hunters include wasps, ladybugs, spiders, and birds.

Orb weaver spiders mainly feed on insects that they catch in the sticky threads of their webs.

A chickadee feeding a hungry brood might collect several hundred caterpillars in a day. However, its chicks or even its eggs might end up in the stomach of a larger bird, such as a magpie, jay, or owl.

Grub for Grab!

Other birds come to feast on the grubs under the bark. Spotted woodpeckers and tree creepers have strong feet for clinging to the trunk and specially-shaped beaks for dragging the grubs out.

Woodpeckers drill holes into the wood to make their nests.

The Oak as Host

Fungi, ferns, and moss are moisture-loving plants that thrive in the shade under the oak tree. Mushrooms and toadstools also grow here, usually in autumn. They feed on the dead leaves and twigs. Nutrients released when they break down the dead material are taken up by the tree roots and used to make new growth.

Even an old, dead oak is a microhabitat. Mites and beetles like this stag beetle feed on the dead wood, while fungi and lichen take over the bark.

Climbing High

Not all plants are useful to the oak. Ivy (below) scrambles up the oak's trunk toward the light, clinging with little suckers called rootlets. As the ivy spreads, it covers the tree's leaves.

Guess What?

Bracket fungus found growing on a dead elm tree in Great Britain in 1995 covered an area as big as a double bed. It's still growing bigger, by about 1.5 inches (3.5 cm) each year.

The silvery Spanish moss that grows on oaks isn't really a moss at all. It's a plant that belongs to the pineapple family.

A Festival of the Morel is held at Elba in the Whitewater Valley, Minnesota, each spring to celebrate these delicious mushrooms that grow in the oak forests there.

This prevents the oak from getting enough light to make food, which can weaken it so much that it may die.

However, ivy does provide safe nesting sites for birds. Its flowers also provide nectar for insects in the autumn.

Other Trees

Broad-Leaved Trees

Most oaks, but not all, are broad-leaved trees: their leaves are broad and flat. Other species of broad-leaved trees include beeches, maples, and fruit trees. All of these are deciduous trees—which means they lose their leaves in winter, blossoming in spring and producing seeds in autumn. However, over 200 kinds of oak are evergreens.

Many varieties of cherry tree are grown for their blossoms as well as their fruit. Japanese cherry trees like this one are ornamental trees, grown almost solely for their beautiful flowers.

The color, scent, and nectar of the apple blossom attract hoverflies, butterflies, and bees.

Insect Attractors

Cherry trees, horse chestnut trees, and apple trees have many more colorful flowers than the oak. This is because their flowers are **pollinated** by insects, not the wind.

Going to Seed

In autumn, the fruits of broad-leaved trees attract many kinds of birds. The birds get a meal, and in turn they help the tree. The seeds inside the fruit pass through the birds and come out in their droppings. In time, new trees may grow from these same seeds.

Chestnuts are protected by a spiky outer covering that helps deter nut-eating predators.

Other Types of Tree

Not all trees are broad-leaved or deciduous. Evergreens are trees that keep their leaves throughout the year. Conifers (cone-bearing trees) are evergreens that have tough needles to survive fierce cold or dry heat. Their sloping and flexible branches allow snow to slip right off them. Birds that feed on their cones include the crossbill, which pokes the seeds out with its specially adapted beak.

(Above) Each pine needle has a thick cuticle— a protective waxy coating that stops it from losing water and drying out.

The pine marten hunts in the branches of pine trees. It eats bird eggs and insects.

26

Tropical Trees

In the tropics, where there is no cold winter season, most trees keep their leaves all year. These trees include palms that bear coconuts and dates, and tropical fruit trees that produce figs, mangoes, and papayas.

The delicious nuts and fruits of tropical trees attract monkeys and birds.

Guess What?

Bristlecone pines, which are native to the Rocky Mountains, live longer than any other type of conifer. One bristlecone in Nevada is about 4,900 years old.

The tropical coco-de-mer, which is native to the Seychelles Islands of the Indian Ocean, produces the biggest fruit of any plant. Its nuts weigh as much as 44 pounds (20 kg) and take 10 years to ripen fully.

A lemur can gorge on as many as 500 figs a week!

The Importance of Trees

Save the Trees!

Like the oak, all trees provide animals and plants with precious food or shelter. Some animals even depend on one particular type of tree for their survival. Koalas, for example, will feed only on eucalyptus leaves.

Trees and Us

Trees are beautiful to look at and they are essential to life, too. Photosynthesis provides much of the oxygen that humans and other animals need to breathe. Many trees produce edible fruits and nuts, including hazelnuts, pine kernels, and apples. They also provide us with timber, one of our most useful natural materials.

Sometimes people hurry to clear away fallen trees, branches, and logs from the forest floor. However, even fallen and dead trees can be a habitat for insects and small mammals as well as for lichen and other plant life.

What We Can Do

We must make sure there are trees for people to enjoy in the future. We must not chop down more than we plant. We must also stop or reduce pollution wherever possible, because it damages trees and the environment on which trees depend for their health.

Two loggers working in a temperate rain forest of the Olympic Peninsula in Washington State.

Guess What?

About 87 percent of the original rain forests of North America have been cut down. A further 7 percent is likely to be felled. The remaining forest may not be large enough to support the wildlife that lives there now.

Only 6 percent of the world's tropical forests are protected by law. The rest is threatened by commercial logging.

In the early 20th century, a fungus called Dutch elm disease destroyed millions of American elms.

Glossary

Dormant: (DOR-muhnt) Not active. An acorn is dormant during the winter, when it is too cold for it to grow.

Fertilize: (FUR-tuh-lize) To make something able to produce fruit, seeds, or offspring.

Germinate: (JUR-muh-nate) To make something sprout and develop.

Hibernation: (HYE-bur-nay-shuhn) A sleeplike state in which some animals exist during the coldest months of the year.

Larva: (LAR-vuh) An insect baby, such as a beetle grub, that looks nothing like its parent.

Lobe: (LOHB) The parts of the edge of an oak leaf that are rounded and stick out.

Nutrient: (NOO-tree-uhnt) A substance that nourishes (feeds) a plant or animal—for example, any of the minerals found in soil.

Pollinate: (POL-uh-nate) To transfer male pollen to female flower parts. Plants might rely on wind, insects, birds, or other animals to move the pollen.

Species: (SPEE-sheez) A type of animal or plant. For example, a red oak roller weevil is a species of weevil.

Temperate: (TEM-pur-it) A climate that varies with the seasons and is not characterized by either the extreme cold of the polar regions or the high temperature and humidity of the tropics.

Further Reading

Aronson, Steven M. L. *Trees: Identified by Leaf, Bark, & Seed.* New York: Workman Publishing Company, 1998.

Boring, Mel. *Birds, Nests, and Eggs.* Pittsburgh, PA: Creative Publishing International, 1998.

Kirkland, Jane. *Take a Backyard Bird Walk.* Stillwater, MN: Stillwater Publishing, 2001.

Stotksy, Sandra. *Trees Are Terrific!* (Ranger Rick's Naturescope Series Vol.1). Broomall, PA: Chelsea House Publishers, 1999.

Websites

http://www.childrensforest.com/
Grow a virtual tree, and learn fascinating facts about trees that will help this virtual tree grow!

http://www.domtar.com/arbre/english/start.htm
Find out anything you want to know about trees, play games, take quizzes, and take a trip through the forest.

Index

acorns 6-8, 11-12, 14-17
apple trees 25
autumn 6-11, 24-25

badgers 13
bats 12, 14
beech trees 24
beetles 16, 22
birds 5-6, 14-15, 20, 25-27
blossom 24-25
broadleaved trees 4, 24-26
bugs 16
butterflies 18-19, 25

camouflage 19
carbon dioxide 8
caterpillars 15, 18-20
catkins 9
cherry trees 24-25
chestnut trees 25
chickadees 20
chlorophyll 8, 10
conifers 26-27
crows 14
cuckoos 21

dead wood 21-22, 28
deciduous trees 24, 26
deer 12

elm trees 23
environment, the 29
evergreens 4, 24, 26

ferns 22
fertilization 9
foxes 13
fruit trees 24-25
fungi 5, 22-23

galls 17
germination 7
growth rings 6

insects 5, 12, 14, 16-17, 25, 28
ivy 5, 23

jays 6, 14, 20

ladybugs 20
leaf litter 5, 11, 16
lichen 22, 28
logging 29 29

magpies 14
mammals 5, 12-13
maple trees 24
mice 12-13
mistletoe 23
moss 22-23
moths 18-19
myths (about trees) 5

nests 14
nutrients 11, 14, 23

oak trees
    age of oaks 4, 6
    bark 11, 16, 19, 22-23
    branches 7-9, 11, 15-16
    flowers 9
    leaves 7-10, 13, 17-19, 23-24
    oak apples 17
    seedlings 7
    shoots 7, 12
    trunk 4, 7, 10, 23
owls 14-15, 20-21
oxygen 8, 28

parasites 23
pheasants 15
photosynthesis 28
pine martens 26
pine needles 26
pollen 9
pollination 25
pollution 29

rabbits 13
raccoons 13
rain forests 29
robins 15
rooks 14
rootlets 23
roots 7, 12-13, 16

spiders 5, 20
spring 7, 8, 24
squirrels 5-6, 12-13
sunlight 4, 8, 10, 23

temperate climates 7
thrushes 15
tortoiseshell butterflies 18
tree
        fruits 27-8
        seeds 25, 27-28
tree creepers 21

vaporer moths 18
voles 12-13

warblers 15
wasps 17, 20
weevils 16-17
winter 6-11, 13, 24
wood lice 16
woodpeckers 14-15, 21
wrens 15